8

FASCINATING SCIENCE PROJECTS

HEAT and ENERGY

Bobbi Searle

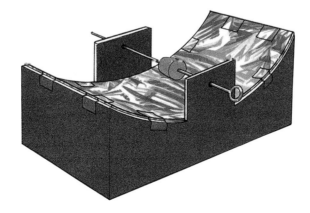

Franklin Watts
London • Sydney

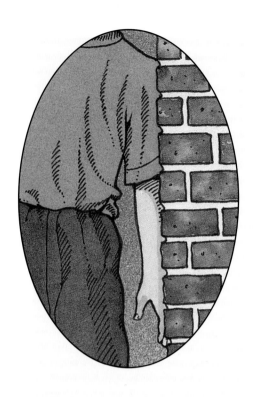

© Aladdin Books Ltd 2001
Produced by
Aladdin Books Ltd
28 Percy Street
London W1P 0LD

ISBN 0–7496–4460–5

First published in Great Britain in 2001 by
Franklin Watts
96 Leonard Street
London
EC2A 4XD

Designers:
Flick, Book design and graphics
Simon Morse

Editor:
Sarah Milan

Illustrators:
Andrew Geeson, Catherine Ward
and Peter Wilks – SGA
Cartoons:
Tony Kenyon – BL Kearley

Consultant:
Bryson Gore

Printed in Belgium

A CIP catalogue record for this book is available
from the British Library.

Contents

Introduction

In this book, the science of heat and energy is explained through a series of fascinating projects and experiments. Each chapter deals with a different topic on heat and energy and contains a major project that is supported by simple experiments, 'Magic panels' and 'Fascinating fact' boxes. At the end of every chapter is an explanation of what has happened and what this means. Projects requiring sharp tools or use of fire should be done under adult supervision.

This states the purpose of the project

METHOD NOTES
Helpful hints on things to remember when carrying out your project.

Materials
In this box is a full list of the items needed to carry out each main project.

1. The steps that describe how to carry out each project are listed clearly as numbered points.
2. Where there are illustrations to help you understand the instructions, the text refers to them as Figure 1, etc.

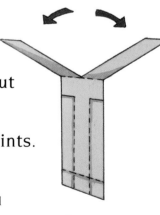

Figure 2

Figure 1

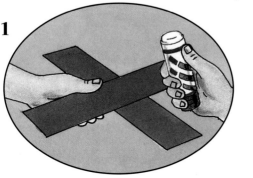

THE AMAZING MAGIC PANEL
This heading states what is happening

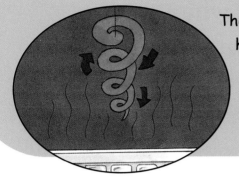

These boxes contain an activity or experiment that has a particularly dramatic or surprising result!

WHY IT WORKS
You can find out exactly what happened here too.

WHAT THIS SHOWS

These boxes, either headed 'What this shows' or 'Why it works', contain an explanation of what happened during your project, and the meaning of the result.

Fascinating facts!
An amusing or surprising fact related to the theme of the chapter.

Where the project involves heating a substance, using a sharp knife or anything else that requires adult supervision, you will see this warning symbol.

The text in these circles links the theme of the topic from one page to the next in the chapter.

What is heat?

Heat is all around us. We feel it when the Sun shines on us or when we do a lot of exercise. It is a form of energy caused by the constant movement of tiny particles called atoms and molecules, which are the building blocks of all things. As molecules move (or vibrate) faster, the material they make up gets hotter. Heat is essential for everything we do. It makes liquids boil and solids melt. Without heat we would not be able to cook our food or even grow it.

Make a thermometer to measure heat

METHOD NOTES
Rub your hands together to warm them before you test out your thermometer.

Materials
- a small see-through plastic bottle
- a see-through drinking straw
- modelling clay
- red food colouring

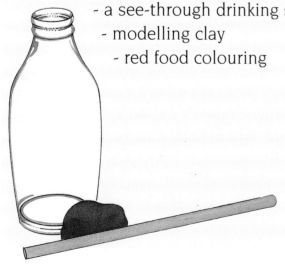

1. Pour some cold tap water into the bottle so it is about a quarter full.
2. Add two or three drops of food colouring and mix it into the water (Figure 1).

Figure 1

6

3. Put the straw into the bottle, but don't let it touch the bottom.

4. Use the modelling clay to seal the neck of the bottle and hold the straw in place (Figure 2).

5. Hold the bottle between your hands for several minutes and watch what happens to the level of liquid in the straw.

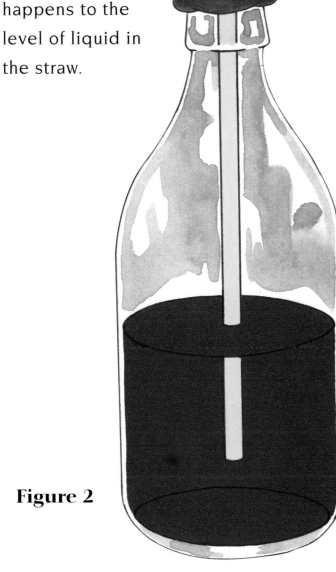

Figure 2

WHY IT WORKS

The air in your bottle expanded when it was warmed by your hands. As the air got hotter, it filled more space in the bottle, leaving less space for the liquid. This forced the liquid up inside the straw.

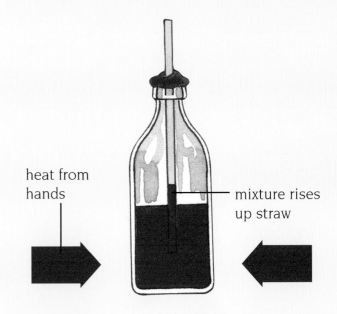

heat from hands

mixture rises up straw

Your bottle is a simple thermometer. A thermometer is an instrument that measures temperature. It usually uses substances like mercury and alcohol, which expand or contract with slight temperature changes.

Thermometers use measurements to tell us how hot or cold it is. Try drawing a scale on your thermometer.

What is heat?

Heat is the energy of moving molecules. We can measure heat (or how fast the molecules are moving) by using a temperature scale. Every substance freezes and boils at a certain temperature.

BOILING AND FREEZING

Put a cupful of plain water in a saucepan and a cupful of very salty water in another saucepan. Time how long it takes for each one to boil and then take the temperature. Try comparing the results. Which one took the longest to boil? Which had the highest boiling point?

Try the experiment again with the same liquids, but this time try testing their freezing points. Put a sample of both into an ice-cube tray and put them in the freezer. Keep checking your samples to see how long it takes each one to freeze. Does the salty water take much longer to freeze than the plain water?

WHY IT WORKS

The salty water takes longer to boil than the pure water and its boiling temperature is higher. This is because the salt molecules stick between the water molecules, making it harder for them to escape as steam and the water to boil.

FREEZING FUN

Push an object into a block of modelling clay to make a mould. Pull the object out and fill the remaining hole with water. Put your mould into a freezer for a few hours. When the water has frozen, push out your sculpture.

LOOK AT THE STATES OF WATER

Water exists as three states of matter – as a solid (ice), a liquid (water) and a gas (steam). It changes state depending on its temperature. When water loses heat, the molecules slow down and create a solid substance – ice. When it is heated to a high enough temperature, the molecules move very fast and escape into the air as steam.

Place some ice in a saucepan and time how long it takes to turn into water and then to boil. Then heat some cold water and time how long it takes to boil. Why does the ice take much longer to boil than the cold water does?

Using an oven glove to protect your hand from the heat, hold a metal spoon above a pan of boiling water or a boiling kettle. The steam will collect on your spoon, cool and turn back into water.

The great escape!
On a mountain top there is much less air pressure. Water boils at a lower temperature. In lower air pressure the water molecules can escape as steam more easily.

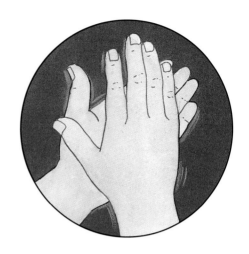

HEATING OUR BODIES

We warm ourselves up by rubbing together parts of our body like our hands or feet. By doing this, we create friction which produces heat. Try rubbing your hands together slowly for 30 seconds and then quickly for 30 seconds. Which made your hands feel warmer?

THE AMAZING SQUIRMING SNAKE
Use convection currents to move your snake

1. Cut out a snake shape from a piece of circular paper. Decorate it as you like.
2. With a needle, make a small hole at the head of the snake and thread a piece of cotton thread through. Tie tightly.
3. Hold the end of the thread and let the snake hang freely. Hold it above a warm heater and watch what happens.

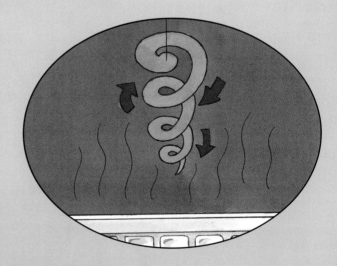

WHY IT WORKS

Warm air is lighter than cold air, so it rises as it gets hotter. This creates waves of air called convection currents. It is these currents that make your snake spin as you hold it above the heater.

HEAT CONDUCTION

Put three different spoons – metal, wooden and plastic – into three glasses or cups of hot water. Leave them all for two minutes. Take them out of the water and feel the handle of each one. Which one is the hottest?

WHY IT WORKS

Some materials are better conductors of heat than others. This means they allow heat to move through them more quickly. When heat travels through a material, the molecules vibrate faster, passing on the heat to other molecules. Metals are good conductors of heat, which is why they are used to make saucepans. The handle of your metal spoon will be the hottest. Materials like wood and plastic are poor conductors. This is why the plastic and wooden spoon handles did not heat up as quickly as the metal one.

Heat is a form of energy – the energy of moving molecules. It can be passed from one substance to another. Different substances can be heated, boiled, cooled and frozen, but some take longer to do this than others. Some materials can conduct heat very quickly, and others take longer.

What is energy?

Energy is what moves, heats and lights everything around us. It is found in different forms and is stored in different ways. Petrol, batteries and food all store energy which most of us use every day. Energy can never be destroyed – it just changes from one form to another. For example, a plant uses the Sun's energy to convert water and carbon dioxide gas into the energy it needs to grow. We eat plants and turn their energy into power to move our muscles.

Demonstrate how air can create a force

METHOD NOTES
Make sure that you use smooth string. Rough string will cause friction and slow your rocket down.

Materials
- a balloon
- a plastic drinking straw
- a long piece of string
- sticky tape
- a chair

1. Tie one end of the string to the back of a chair.
2. Thread the other end of the string through the straw (Figure 1).

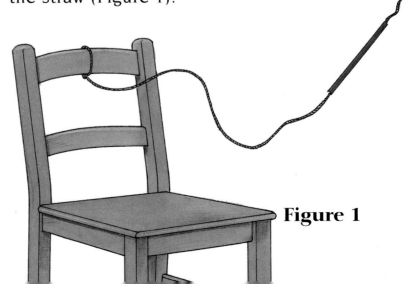

Figure 1

3. Pull the string tight and tie it to another support in the room, such as a doorknob or handle.

4. Blow up the balloon but don't tie it. Pinch the end instead and tape it to the straw (Figure 2).

5. Let go of the balloon and watch what happens.

WHY IT WORKS

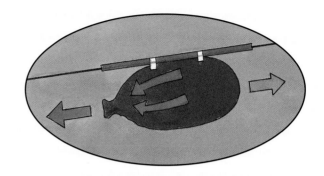

When you let go of the balloon, the air inside is forced out at high speed. This creates 'thrust' – a force that moves objects forwards. Because the straw is able to move easily along the string, your 'rocket' will move smoothly until all the air comes out of the balloon. Try the experiment with rough string or twine and watch what happens this time.

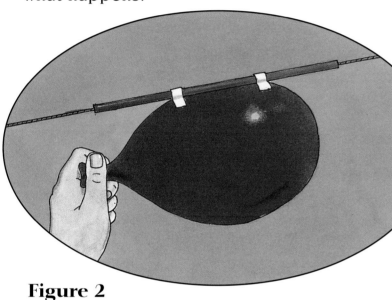

Figure 2

Careless cars!
Even the most efficient car uses only about 40 per cent of the energy stored in its fuel. The rest is used to overcome friction or is changed into heat energy. The heat goes into the air and is no help in making the car move!

What is energy?

One of the main forms of energy is heat. This can be useful in many ways – from heating a furnace, where steel is made, to keeping the water warm in your house for a nice, hot shower.

CREATE HEAT FROM ELECTRICITY

Half fill a glass with cold water and measure the temperature. Tightly wrap a long piece of insulated copper wire around the bottom half of the thermometer, leaving the ends sticking out. Put the thermometer in the water. Connect the two ends of wire to the terminals of a large battery. Now watch what happens to the temperature of the water.

THE AMAZING BOUNCING BALLS
See how energy transfers from one object to another

1. Drop a ping-pong ball and a golf ball on the ground and see how high they both bounce.
2. Now hold the ping-pong ball on top of the golf ball in one hand and drop them together, so they hit the ground as shown in the picture on the right.

WHY IT WORKS
The ping-pong ball bounces higher than normal. This is because, as both balls hit the ground, the energy from the golf ball is transferred to the ping-pong ball.

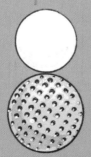

WHY IT WORKS
By connecting wires to a battery, you have made an electrical circuit. As the electricity whizzes through the circuit, it creates heat. The heat goes into the water and the temperature rises.

SHOW HOW A CHEMICAL CHANGE PUSHES A BOAT FORWARD

1. Mould the shape of a boat out of clay, or use several sheets of tin foil to make a lighter boat. Make high sides so that water can't get in (Figure 1).

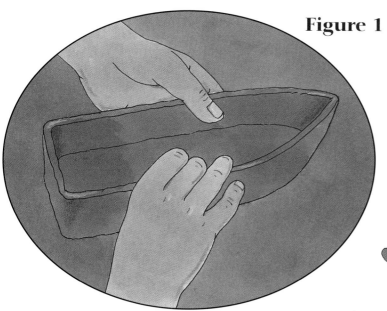

Figure 1

WHY IT WORKS

Once the boat is floating, water slowly begins to come into it through the small hole. The water mixes with the baking powder and dissolves. A chemical change takes place, producing carbon dioxide gas bubbles, which go into the water at the back of the boat. Energy in the baking powder has been changed into energy that pushes the boat forwards. When all the baking powder has dissolved, the boat will stop moving.

Figure 2

2. Pierce the clay or foil to make a small hole in the bottom of the boat at the tail end.
3. Place a heap of baking powder in the tail end of the boat over the hole (Figure 2).
4. Carefully place the boat in a bowl of water and watch what happens.

We have seen that energy can be found in different forms – it causes movement, it produces heat and it can be transferred to other objects. Whatever form it takes, it contains the ability to make something 'happen' – without energy, the world would literally come to a standstill.

The human body

Human beings are the perfect example of heat and energy working together. Our bodies need energy to stay alive. We get this from the food we eat. Our bodies convert these raw materials into the energy we need to walk, talk and keep warm. The more energy we burn up – by hard physical or mental exercise – the more food we need as fuel.

Show how muscles work in pairs

METHOD NOTES
Make sure that the lollipop sticks are clean and dry before you stick tape to them.

Materials
- two lollipop sticks
- two elastic bands
- a craft knife
- a paper fastener
- sticky tape

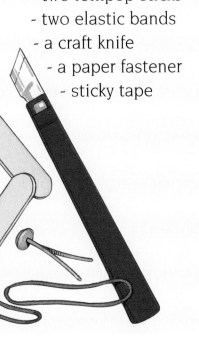

1. Using the craft knife, carefully make a hole in one end of each lollipop stick. Don't do it too close to the end.
2. Place the lollipop sticks on top of each other and thread a paper fastener through both (Figure 1). Straighten out each 'leg' of the paper fastener to hold the sticks together.
3. Cut the two elastic bands so that each one is just a long piece of elastic.

Figure 1

Figure 2

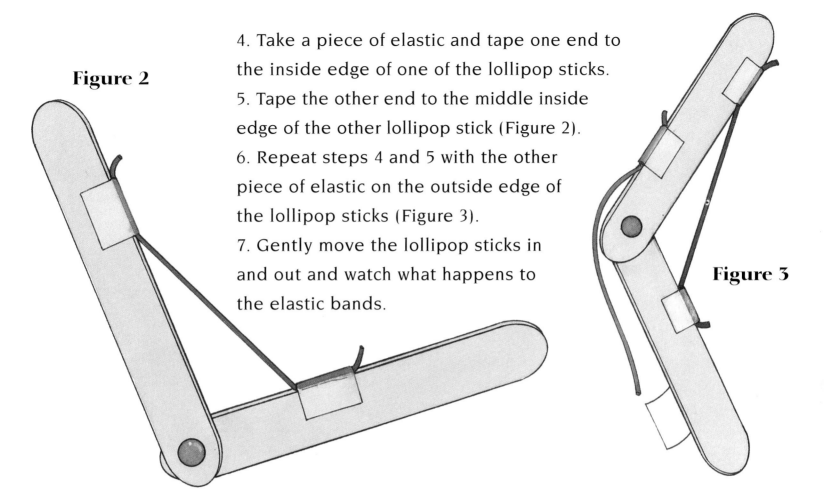

4. Take a piece of elastic and tape one end to the inside edge of one of the lollipop sticks.

5. Tape the other end to the middle inside edge of the other lollipop stick (Figure 2).

6. Repeat steps 4 and 5 with the other piece of elastic on the outside edge of the lollipop sticks (Figure 3).

7. Gently move the lollipop sticks in and out and watch what happens to the elastic bands.

Figure 3

WHAT THIS SHOWS

The muscles in your body stretch and contract (shorten) like the elastic bands. When the biceps muscle on the inside of your upper arm contracts, it raises your arm. Another muscle on the outside (the triceps) pulls your arm back to its original position. Feel them work as a pair as you bend and straighten your arm.

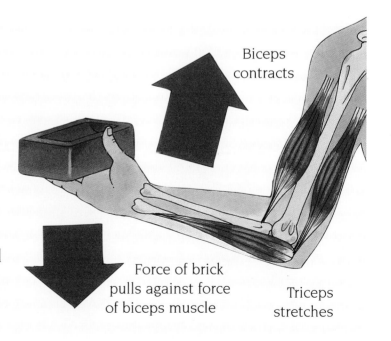

Biceps contracts

Force of brick pulls against force of biceps muscle

Triceps stretches

Our bodies need heat to function, but they are put in danger if they are surrounded by too much heat or cold. Our sense of touch tells us whether we are too hot or too cold for our own safety.

The human body

TRICK YOUR SENSE OF TOUCH

Fill one bowl with cold water, one with hot tap water and one with half of each. Now put your left hand in the hot water and your right hand in the cold water. Leave them in the water for two minutes. Now put both your hands in the bowl with warm water in it. See how your hands feel now.

WHY IT WORKS

Your right hand is used to the temperature of cold water and thinks the warm water is hot by comparison. It works the other way round for your left hand. To this hand, the water feels cold.

Keeping cool!
If you do some exercise, your body temperature stays constant even though you feel warm! This is because your body has a clever system for keeping you cool – sweating. This takes heat away from your body.

THE 'FOOL YOUR ARM' TRICK
Use energy to fool your muscles

As well as fooling your body about heat, you can also fool it about the amount of energy it needs to use.
1. Stand next to a wall and push your arm as hard as you can against it for one minute.
2. Now stand away from the wall and watch as your arm magically starts to rise.

WHY IT WORKS
By pushing against the wall with your arm, your muscles are using a lot of energy. When you step away, they continue to work, so they raise your arm, even though you feel as if you aren't doing anything yourself.

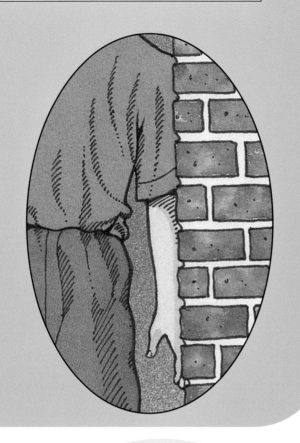

COUNTING CALORIES

We must all eat food every day to get the energy we need to survive. The energy in the food we eat and the liquid we drink is measured in kilocalories (kcal). Have a look at the labels on the food you eat in one day and add up how much energy, or calories, you have eaten.

Without our source of energy (food), humans would not be able to live. By burning up this energy, we are able to function and to make our own source of heat. Our bodies have clever ways of coping with too much heat or cold.

Wind power

Although we get most of our energy from coal, oil and gas, there are lots of other ways of producing it. Wind power is one way. Wind power is a renewable source of energy and can create electricity to light our houses and run our factories. Large groups of modern windmills – or turbines – placed in windy locations harness the power of the wind to make electricity.

Make an anemometer to measure wind speed

METHOD NOTES
Cut off the rolled edges of your cups before you start – this will make them lighter.

Materials
- four small paper cups
- thick card or cardboard
- a pencil with a rubber on the end
- a drawing pin
- modelling clay
- some glue or a stapler
- paint and a paintbrush
- scissors

1. Paint the outside of one of the cups and leave it to dry.

2. Cut out two strips of cardboard and glue or staple them together in a cross shape (Figure 1).

3. Glue or staple the cups to the ends of the cardboard strips. Make sure the cups face the same direction (Figure 2).

Figure 1

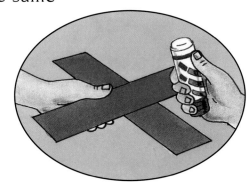
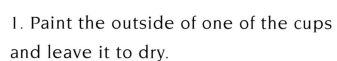

4. Push the drawing pin through the centre of the cardboard cross and into the rubber on the end of your pencil (Figure 3).

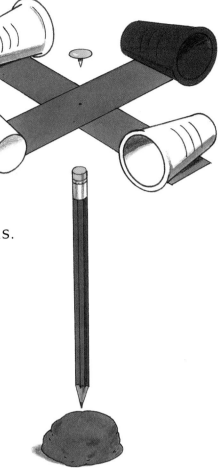

Figure 3

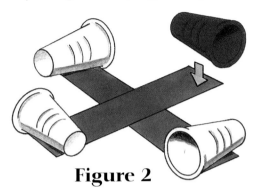

5. Push the point of the pencil into a ball of modelling clay.

6. Place your anemometer outside and watch what happens.

Figure 2

WHY IT WORKS

An anemometer is a device that tells you how fast the wind is blowing. The force of the wind blowing into the open cups causes them to turn. Count the number of times the coloured cup spins round in one minute (its revolution). The stronger the wind and the lighter the cups, the faster they will move. The force of the wind can be expressed in kilometres per hour.

Hold tight!
Winds can be extremely strong. Hurricanes are the most powerful winds of all. They can blow at up to 240 km/h, ripping up trees, houses and anything else that gets in their way!

Wind power

MAKE YOUR OWN KITE

You will need two pieces of dowelling, a ball of string, old sheeting, a bin liner, scissors and tape.

1. Use string to join the two pieces of dowelling tightly together in a cross shape (Figure 1).

2. Place the frame onto a bin liner and cut out a shape slightly bigger than the frame. Fold the edges over the frame and tape down (Figure 2).

3. Cut some old sheeting into a strip two centimetres wide and twice as long as your kite. Attach it to the bottom of your kite as a tail.

Figure 1

4. Attach two long pieces of string to the crossbars of your kite and tie them to the end of a ball of string (Figure 3).

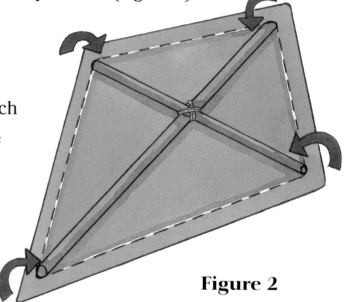

Figure 2

5. Wait for a windy day to go and fly your kite.

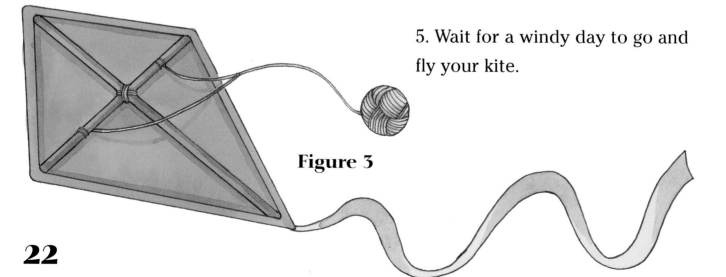

Figure 3

SEE HOW A WINDMILL WORKS

1. Draw a dot in the centre of a square piece of card. Draw a line from each corner towards the dot but stop halfway (Figure 1).
2. Cut along each of these lines. Fold each left-hand corner towards the dot (Figure 2).
3. Using a drawing pin or nail, join all the corners in the centre. Then push the pin through the card into a piece of dowelling (Figure 3).
4. Put your windmill in a windy place and watch as the wind catches the sails and spins them round.

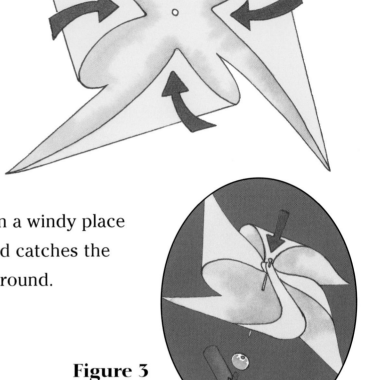

Figure 2

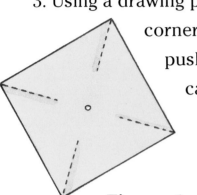

Figure 1

Figure 3

MAKE A WIND CHIME

Collect different objects to make a wind chime – shells and metal things work well. Cut out a large circle from strong card. Make some holes around the outside of the circle and hang your objects from them with string. Use string to hang your wind chime somewhere windy. Listen to the sounds.

The wind is a powerful, if unpredictable, force of nature that has been used by humans to generate power for a long time. We harness its power in other ways too – for making sounds to scare birds away from crops and for many sporting activities.

Water power

Water is one of the most powerful sources of energy on the planet. However, it must be harnessed in the right way. Hydroelectric dams produce almost 20 per cent of the world's electricity. Water is captured in a huge reservoir and fed through a turbine to create electricity. This is mostly produced in areas with large rivers and lakes like Scandinavia and North America.

Explore how water turns a turbine

METHOD NOTES
Make sure your water wheel spins freely inside the bottle before you try it out.

Materials
- a large see-through plastic bottle
- a cork
- a craft knife
- a skewer or a sharp pencil
- a drinking straw

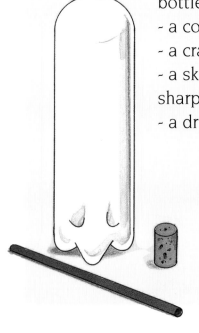

1. Carefully cut out a window from the side of the bottle with the craft knife (Figure 1). Make sure you cut this out as one complete piece (see step 4).

2. Using the point of the knife, make two holes on either side of the window, large enough to thread a straw through.

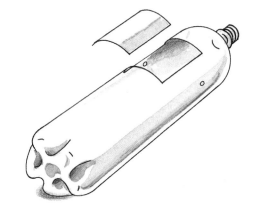

Figure 1

24

Figure 2

3. Using a skewer or a sharp pencil, make a hole all the way through the middle of a cork. Thread the straw through the cork (Figure 2).

4. Cut the plastic that you cut out of the bottle into six equal pieces. Push these into the cork at regular intervals (Figure 3).

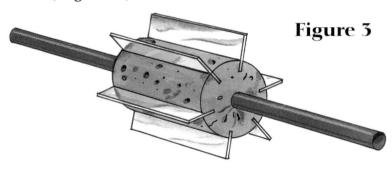

Figure 3

5. Thread the ends of the straw through the holes in the bottle on either side of the window.

6. Place the neck of the bottle underneath a flowing tap and watch what happens (Figure 4).

WHY IT WORKS

The water wheel – or turbine – spins round as the weight of the water hits the blades. As one blade is pushed down, the wheel turns and the water falls onto the next blade. As long as the water keeps flowing, the wheel will keeps turning. Experiment with turning on the tap at different speeds – does the water wheel turn faster or slower? As the bottle gets full of water, tip it out and start again.

Figure 4

Water power

MAKE A WATER JET

Cut off the bottom of a plastic bottle. Seal the mouth with modelling clay and push a straw through the clay into the bottle. Fit another straw to the end of the first straw to form a U-shape (Figure 1). Pierce two holes at either end of a plastic tray. Turn the bottle upside down and feed the straw tube through the holes. Seal the bottle over one of the holes using modelling clay. Place the tray in a bowl, fill the bottle with liquid and watch what happens (Figure 2).

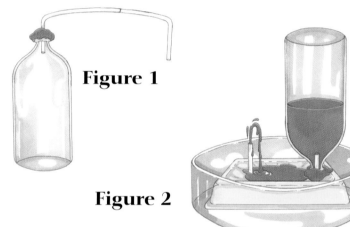

Figure 1

Figure 2

WHY IT WORKS

The water 'fountain' is caused by the weight of the water in the upturned bottle. This weight causes a build-up of pressure. The more water there is in the bottle, the greater the pressure and the higher the fountain will soar.

What a spark!
Niagara Falls is the largest producer of electric power in the world! Half of its huge amount of flowing water drives turbines to make power for the US and Canada.

A BOAT POWERED BY HEAT AND WATER

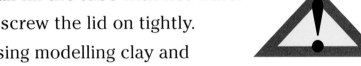

Figure 1

1. Punch a small hole in the lid of a lightweight metal tube that is sealed at one end, such as a cigar tube, using a hammer and small nail (Figure 1). If your tube doesn't have a lid, tightly seal the end with a cork with a small hole through it.

2. Half fill the tube with hot water and screw the lid on tightly.

3. Using modelling clay and pipe cleaners,

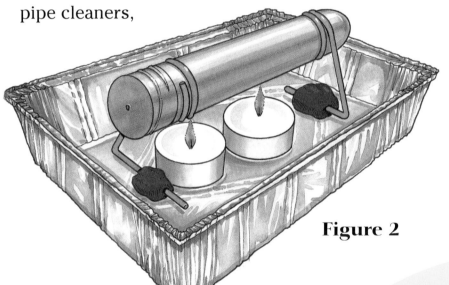

Figure 2

fix the tube to the bottom of a foil tray (Figure 2).

4. Place two candles beneath the tube, as close as possible.

5. Put your 'boat' in water. Now light the candles and watch what happens to your boat.

WHY IT WORKS

The flame from the candles heats the water inside the tube until it begins to boil. The water then changes into steam, which takes up more space than liquid water. It escapes backwards out of the small hole in the lid. This pushes the boat forwards.

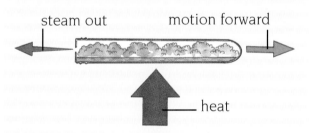

steam out · motion forward · heat

Water power, the force of moving or falling water, can be an effective way of generating electricity. In a steam engine, heat is changed to moving energy. Water is heated until it expands as steam. The force of the steam can be used to power a boat or a steam train.

Solar energy

Energy from the Sun is called solar energy. It reaches us in the form of heat and light. Solar energy is the reason for the existence of life on Earth. Without it plants would not grow and animals would starve. Scientists are exploring ways of harnessing solar energy for uses such as powering engines and heating homes in cold weather.

See how solar energy can cook food

METHOD NOTES
Choose something that won't take too long to cook – marshmallows are perfect.

Materials
- a shoe box
- tin foil
- a wooden or metal skewer
- thin card
- something to cook

1. Cut the shoe box into the shape shown in Figure 1, and make a hole in the centre of the raised flaps.
2. Cut out a piece of card to fit over the opening of the box (but not the flaps) and cover it with foil, shiny side outwards (Figure 2).

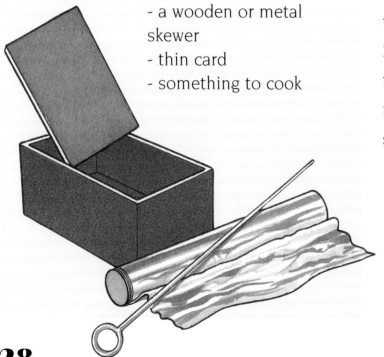

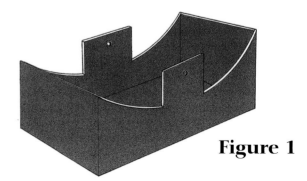

Figure 1

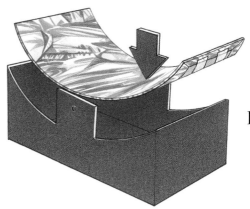

Figure 2

3. Tape the card onto the box.

4. Thread your skewer through one hole, put some food onto your skewer, then thread the skewer through the other hole (Figure 3).

6. Place your solar oven in the Sun and leave your food to cook.

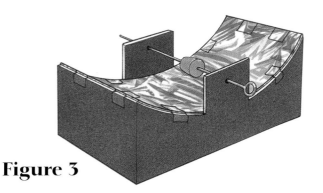

Figure 3

WHY IT WORKS

The Sun's rays are very powerful and contain a lot of energy. The tin foil reflects these rays like a mirror and, because of the way the card is curved, concentrates them onto the food you are cooking. The heat warms the food and, after a while, cooks it all the way through to the middle.

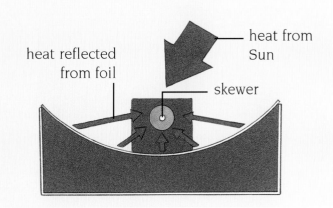

heat reflected from foil

heat from Sun

skewer

Speed from the Sun!
Solar-powered cars use the energy of the Sun and solar cells to create and store energy. Some of these cars have travelled across Australia (3,000 km) using only the power of the Sun!

Solar energy

CAPTURE THE SUN'S HEAT

Fill two identical jam jars with two cups of cold water. Place five ice cubes in each. Put one jar inside a plastic bag and seal it. Place both of the jars outside in a sunny place for one hour. After the hour is up, check to see if the ice has melted and measure the temperature of the water in each jar.

WHY IT WORKS

In hot sunshine, the air trapped inside the plastic bag becomes warm. The heat builds up and melts the ice. The heat escapes from the other jar, so the ice takes longer to melt. Greenhouses work in this way.

COOK A BRICK IN THE SUN

Mix four handfuls of soil and straw together (clay-like soil may work better than sandy soil). Add enough water to make the mixture wet but not runny. Cut the bottom out of a small box (Figure 1). Place the box on a piece of cardboard and pour in the mixture. Leave it in the Sun to dry then take it out of the box (Figure 2). The energy from the Sun will bake your brick until it is strong enough to build with.

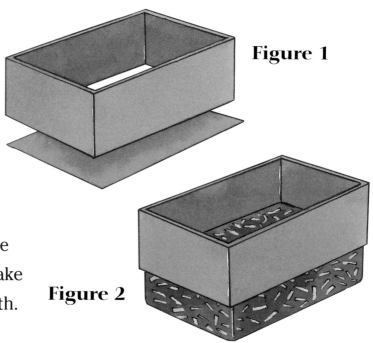

Figure 1

Figure 2

30

THE AMAZING INVISIBLE INK
Use lemon juice and the power of the Sun

1. Cut a lemon in half and squeeze the juice into a glass or cup.
2. Using a toothpick as your pen, dip it into the juice and write a message onto a piece of white paper. Don't use too much juice.
3. Leave the paper to dry in the Sun and watch what happens to your secret message.

WHY IT WORKS
The heat from the Sun causes the lemon juice to dry and go brown. Now you can read what is written on the paper.

SOLAR PRINTING

Choose some objects you want to print – leaves and flowers work well. Arrange them on a piece of dark-coloured card. Leave the card in direct sunlight for three days. Then lift your items off the paper. The Sun fades the paper, but under your items, the paper will be the original colour.

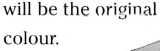

We have seen how the energy from the Sun is essential for life on Earth. It provides vital heat and light, but it can also be harnessed to do jobs such as powering cars. Scientists hope to use more of the Sun's energy to create clean and cheap solar energy.

Hidden energy

Energy isn't just stored in batteries. Take a look around you and you'll discover that it is hidden in the most unusual things. From fruit and vegetables to the cereal you eat for breakfast in the morning, energy is all around you. Finding hidden energy is quite simple – it is inside everything that exists – the difficult part is making it work for you.

Discover energy inside a lemon

METHOD NOTES
Roll the lemon between your hand and a table before you start to soften it up a bit.

Materials
- a lemon
- a steel paperclip
- a small length of copper tubing
- two lengths of insulated copper wire
- a small light bulb (from a torch or penlight)

1. Open out your steel paperclip so that it is straight and push one end of the paperclip into one side of the lemon.

2. Carefully push one end of the copper tube into the opposite side of the lemon (Figure 1).

Figure 1

3. Wrap the end of one length of wire around the top of the straightened paperclip. Wrap the end of the other length of wire around the top of the copper tube.
4. Hold the other two ends of the wire onto the bottom of a small light bulb (Figure 2). Watch what happens to the light bulb.

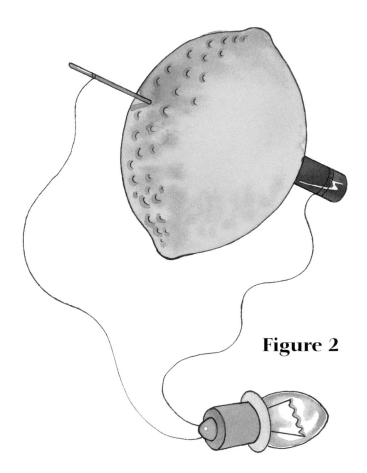

Figure 2

WHY IT WORKS

The lemon juice reacts with the two different metals – copper and steel – and creates electricity. The lemon juice can conduct the electricity between the two metals. When you attach the wires, you make an electric circuit and the current travels from the lemon battery, through the wires and lights the bulb.

You can also try this experiment with another citrus fruit or a potato.

Hot stuff!
Sometimes when you mix two substances together, a chemical reaction takes place. This can produce energy in the form of heat. Mixing water with plaster of Paris (used for sculpture) gives off heat.

Hidden energy

There are different ways of finding the energy stored inside things – one way is by heating a substance, another is by mixing substances together.

POPCORN POWER

Heat some popcorn kernels in a saucepan with a small amount of oil. Put the lid on and wait until all the popcorn has popped. Look at a kernel. What has changed? The water inside each one expands as it is heated and explodes, turning the kernel inside out.

THE EXPLODING FILM CANISTER
Use a chemical reaction to create gas

1. Put a teaspoon of vinegar into an empty plastic film canister.
2. Wrap up a teaspoon of bicarbonate of soda in some tissue paper.

3. Drop the tissue paper package into the film canister and quickly put the top on.
4. Stand back and watch what happens. It may take a while, so be patient and don't take off the lid.

WHY IT WORKS
When the bicarbonate of soda dissolves in the vinegar, a chemical reaction takes place. This produces carbon dioxide gas, which slowly builds up inside the canister. The pressure from the gas blows off the lid.

SEE THE ENERGY IN A PEANUT

1. Carefully push the blunt end of a needle into a cork. Push the other end of the needle into a peanut.
2. Pierce two sides of a tin can with a skewer and put a little cold water in it. Rest the skewer across two bricks just above the peanut (Figure 1). Measure the water temperature.
3. Light the peanut with a match. Place two more bricks around it (Figure 2).

Figure 1

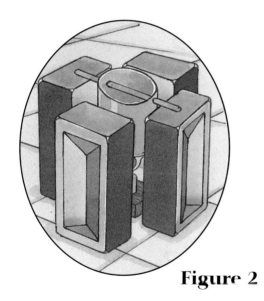

Figure 2

4. When the peanut burns out, measure the temperature of the water again.

WHY IT WORKS

The peanut contains hidden energy. When you set it alight, the oils in the peanut burn and the energy is released and converted into heat. This heat raises the temperature of the water.

Energy is hidden all around us, but it is often difficult to get at. Different substances react together in different ways to produce energy. Scientists are still exploring ways of releasing and using that energy.

On the move

Can you imagine what it would be like without cars or trains, boats or planes? It would take a long time to get anywhere using just the power of your legs. Without energy, none of these machines would exist. We use the stored energy of fuels and batteries to power our everyday transport. Even sailing boats use the energy of the wind to push them along. So you see, energy really is on the move.

Discover how wind can power a racer

METHOD NOTES
If you can't find dowelling, try thin plastic straws instead.

Materials
- a cardboard tube
- a sharp pencil
- two lengths of dowelling (to fit inside cotton reels)
- four cotton reels
- a paper napkin
- three lollipop sticks
- glue

1. Using the point of a pencil, make two holes that go from one side of the cardboard tube through to the other. Make the holes at either end of the tube and position them just below the halfway point (see Figure 1).

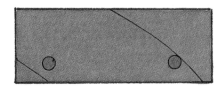

Figure 1

Figure 2

2. Thread a piece of dowelling through each set of holes.

3. Push a cotton reel onto the end of each piece of dowelling – these are your wheels (Figure 2).

4. Make a small hole in the top of the cardboard tube and push through a lollipop stick as a mast.

5. Make a sail using the paper napkin and two lollipop sticks. Glue the sail onto the mast.

6. Use a hairdryer or blow hard behind the sail and watch what happens to your racer (Figure 3).

WHY IT WORKS

The sail of your racer catches the 'wind' that you blow behind it. The force of the wind pushes the sail, which pushes the racer forwards on its wheels. Without wind, your racer would not move at all. Try blowing the wind from a different angle.

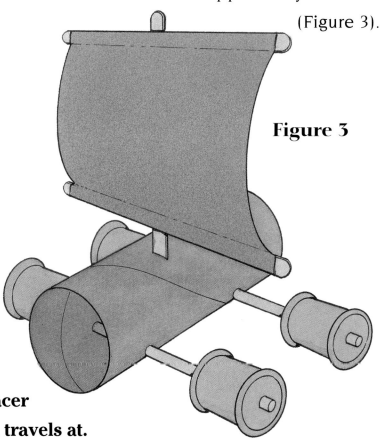

Figure 3

You can experiment with the design of your racer as much as you like. Adjust the size of your sail – does a big sail make it go faster than a small sail? The weight of the racer may make a difference to the speed it travels at. Try making a heavy racer from a shoe box. Can it go as fast? You can also try different ways to move the racer. Can you find a way to use the energy of a twisted elastic band or a balloon?

Wind and water energy make things move, but energy can also be stored. An elastic band can store energy and then release it to move a paddleboat or tank.

On the move

MAKE A PADDLEBOAT

Cut off the tip of two matchsticks and tape them to either side of a matchbox drawer. Push the drawer back into the cover so the matchsticks are sticking out. Stretch a small elastic band across both matchsticks and slot a piece of cardboard in-between. Wind the boat up by twisting the cardboard towards you a few times. Place the paddleboat in some water and let it go.

WHY IT WORKS

As the elastic band unwinds, there is enough energy in it to turn the paddle. The turning paddle pushes against the water and propels the boat forwards.

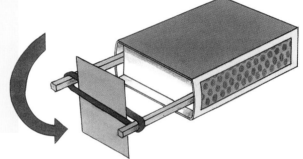

THE AMAZING ROLLING TIN
Use an elastic band to produce energy

1. Ask an adult to pierce two holes in the lid and bottom of an old paint tin.
2. Cut a large elastic band so it is a single strip of elastic.
3. Thread the elastic through the holes, crossing it over in the middle.
4. Tie a nut to the elastic where it crosses over. Then knot the elastic at the lid end.
5. Roll the tin forwards gently.

WHY IT WORKS

Your tin rolls back to you. This is because the heavy weight of the nut pulls it down below the elastic. This means the elastic becomes twisted when you push the tin forwards. The tin rolls back on its own, powered by the energy in the elastic.

TWIST AN ELASTIC BAND TO MAKE A MOVING TANK

1. Thread an elastic band through a cotton reel. Tape half a match to one end of the reel, looping it first through the elastic band (Figure 1).

2. Cut a thin section of candle and make a hole through the middle of it with a pencil.

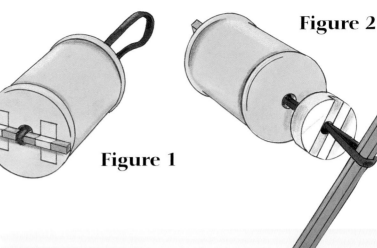

Figure 2

Figure 1

WHY IT WORKS

As you wind up the tank, you are twisting the elastic band inside the reel. When you let it go, the elastic band unwinds, releasing its stored energy. The taped end cannot move, so the other end with the pencil in it turns instead. The pencil pushes against the table or floor and the tank moves.

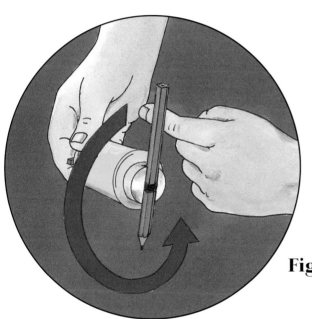

Figure 3

3. Thread the elastic loop through the candle then put a pencil through the loop (Figure 2).

4. Turn the pencil to wind up your tank (Figure 3).

5. Now watch your tank move.

One of the main uses of energy is to make things move. There are many ways of generating this energy: by using renewable sources like wind and water, by converting fuels like oil into energy to power moving vehicles and by using stored energy, such as that found in elastic bands.

All around you

Natural energy is all around you and can be found in all living things. It just needs to be released. Birds use the power of the wind to save their own energy and travel a great distance without too much effort. Plants and seeds use solar energy to help them grow and they use the energy of the wind to help them spread their seeds. The power of the Sun can also be used to produce clean drinking water in the driest desert or the saltiest beach.

Make a tap using the Sun's energy

METHOD NOTES
Make sure you choose a sunny day to do this experiment.

Materials
- a cup or glass
- some large pebbles
- a bin liner

1. Dig a small, deep hole in a sunny part of the garden (remember to ask permission first). Alternatively, you could try this experiment next time you are at a sandy beach.

2. Place a small cup or glass at the bottom of the hole.

3. Stretch a plastic bin liner across the top of the hole and weight down the edges with pebbles or small rocks.

Figure 1

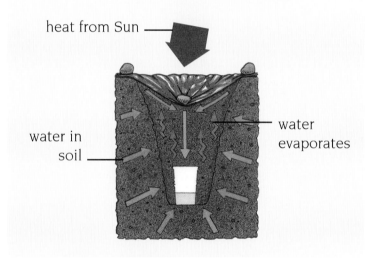

WHY IT WORKS

The heat of the Sun warms the soil or sand under the plastic sheet. This causes some of the water that is naturally stored in the soil or sand to evaporate. The water rises, collects on the plastic sheet, runs down to the middle point and drips into the cup.

heat from Sun

water in soil

water evaporates

4. Place a medium-sized pebble in the middle of the bin liner so that the plastic dips down slightly (Figure 1).
5. Leave your cup in the hole overnight (or as long as possible at the beach) then check to see what has happened.

Rock frying pans!
In some countries, the heat of the Sun is so strong that rocks can become as hot as the stove on your cooker. They get so hot, in fact, that you could fry an egg on them!

All around you

Nature has evolved to work efficiently with the natural sources of energy that are all around us. Some of the best human inventions have been inspired by birds, animals or plants.

LEARN HOW A SYCAMORE SEED FLIES

1. Copy the template in Figure 1 onto a piece of paper. Make it as big as you like. Then cut along all the solid lines.

2. Following the dotted line, fold section A towards you and section B away from you (Figure 2).

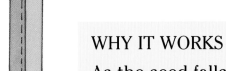

Figure 2

3. Still following the dotted lines, fold section D over section C so they overlap (Figure 3).

4. Now fold up the bottom along the dotted line and attach a paperclip for weight (Figure 4).

5. Hold your sycamore seed high above your head. Then let go of it and watch what happens.

Figure 3

Figure 1

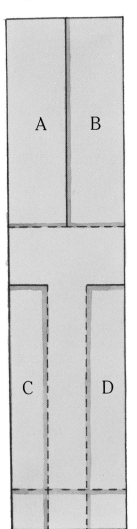

A   B

C   D

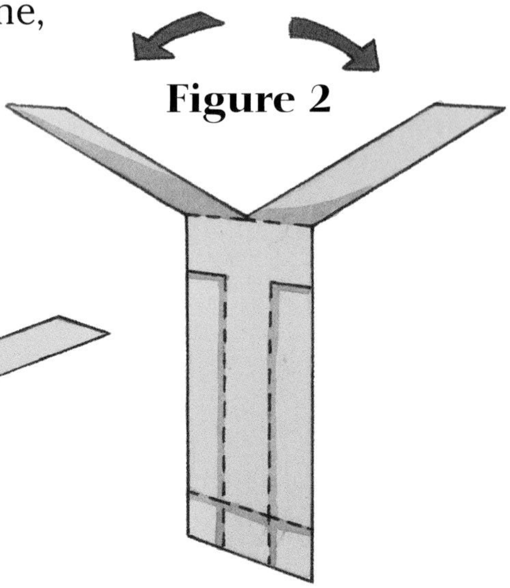

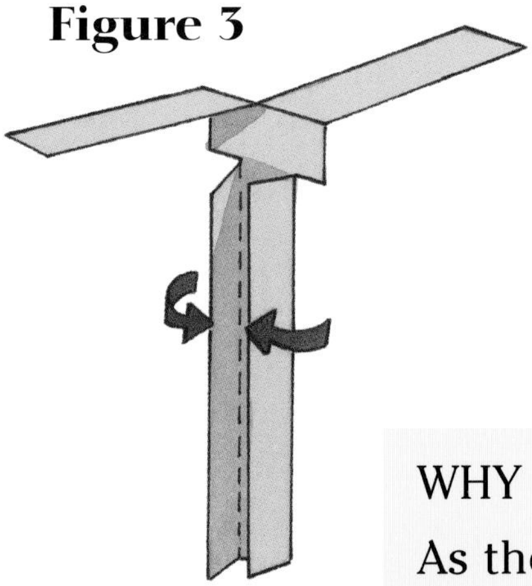

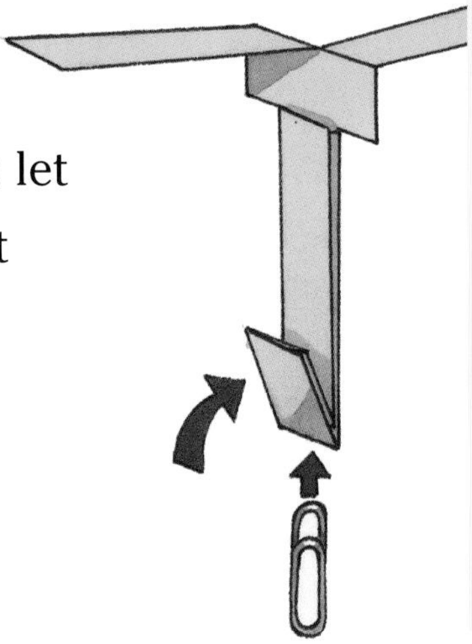

WHY IT WORKS

As the seed falls, air pushes against the blades, making them spin. The spinning blades move the seed through the air. The seed then has a better chance of finding somewhere to grow away from the tree.

Figure 4

SEE HOW THINGS GLIDE

1. Draw a line down the middle of an A4 sheet of paper. Measure 9.5 cm down each side and draw a line joining the middle line. Fold the top corners down along these lines (Figure 1).

2. Now measure 14 cm down each long side and draw a line joining the middle line again. Fold along these lines too (Figure 2).

3. Measure 6.5 cm up from the bottom edge of each side and draw a line towards the pointed end. Fold your glider in half down the middle, away from you. Fold the two sides towards you along the lines (Figure 3).

4. Tape the wings together (Figure 4). Now throw your glider.

WHY IT WORKS

The glider flies so well because of its streamlined shape. Air flows easily over it and does not slow it down. Gliders use rising currents of warm air – thermals – to stay up in the air without engines. Because warm air is lighter than cold air, it rises upwards, taking the glider with it. Birds float upwards in the same way to save energy. The albatross can travel for days without flapping its wings.

Figure 1

Figure 2

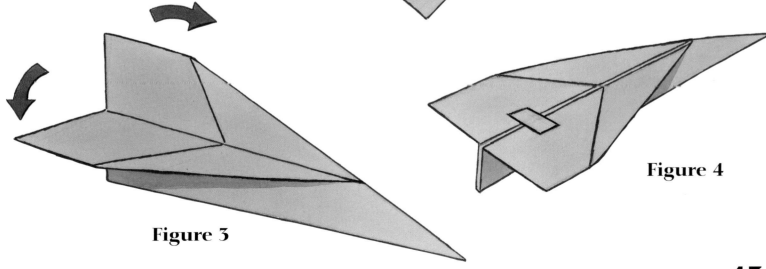

Figure 3

Figure 4

43

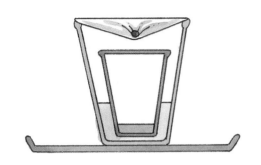

USE SOLAR ENERGY TO PURIFY WATER

Fill a large glass a third full with salty water, then put a small plastic cup in it so that it floats on top of the water. Stretch plastic food wrap over the top of the glass and secure it with an elastic band. Place a stone in the middle of the wrap so it dips. Leave outside in the Sun on top of a metal baking tray and check the next morning.

WHY IT WORKS

Heat from the Sun makes the water inside the glass evaporate, leaving the salt behind. Tiny droplets of pure water then collect on the plastic and drip into the small cup.

THE AMAZINGLY COOL FRIDGE
Use water and a clay pot to keep your drink cool

1. Soak a clay flowerpot in a bucket of water overnight.
2. Fill a large bowl with cold water and place a can of drink in it.
3. Put the flowerpot upside down over the top of the can so that it sits in the bowl of water.
4. Place a small stone over the hole in the flowerpot.
5. Leave in the Sun for a few hours. What happens to the temperature of the can?

WHY IT WORKS

The Sun causes water on the surface of the clay pot to evaporate, causing a cooling effect. The pot keeps soaking up more water from the bowl for the Sun to evaporate, so your can of soft drink stays cool, even though the Sun is beating down. Kitchen refrigerators also operate on the principle of evaporation.

What a high jump!
Did you know that fleas can leap up to twenty times their own height? The human equivalent would be someone jumping over 35 metres into the air.

WATCH A BEAN GROW USING STORED ENERGY AND SOLAR ENERGY

Dampen a piece of kitchen paper with water and place it on a saucer. Soak a bean overnight and put it on top of the paper. Place the saucer in a dark place and watch what happens. After a few days, the bean should begin to grow. It is using the energy stored inside it to feed it for the first few days. After that, put it on a sunny windowsill. There it will use energy from the Sun to help it make its own food.

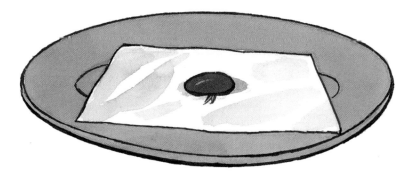

We have discovered that energy is all around us in nature. Birds and seeds use the power of the wind for movement, and have inspired some of the best human designs. Plants use solar energy and their own naturally stored energy to grow. All living things, including us, use energy to move and to function.

Glossary

Conduction

Conduction is the way in which heat energy travels through a substance from one vibrating molecule to another.

Contract

When something contracts, it shrinks in size.

Convection

Convection is when heat is moved through a gas or liquid because the heated parts of the gas or liquid move to cooler parts.

Dissolving

Dissolving happens when two substances such as salt and water combine completely. When one substance dissolves in another, the result is a solution.

Electric charge

An electric charge is a stored amount of electricity.

Electric circuit

An electric circuit is the path around which an electric current flows.

Electric current

An electric current is a flow of electric charge.

Evaporation

Evaporation is what happens when a liquid changes to a gas. Heat speeds up evaporation.

Expand

When something expands, it swells or increases in size.

Force

A force is something that pushes or pulls on an object.

Friction

Friction is the rubbing together of two surfaces. It turns moving energy into heat. In many engines oil is used to reduce friction.

Harness

When you harness something like water power, you control and make use of it for a purpose such as creating electricity.

Hydroelectric power

Hydroelectric power is electricity created by using the power of moving water to turn turbine blades. These drive an electric generator which produces electricity.

Kilocalories

A kilocalorie (often called a calorie) is a measure of energy in food. A teaspoon of sugar has 16 calories.

Molecules

All substances are made of molecules. A molecule is the smallest particle of a substance that exists on its own. Molecules are made up of atoms.

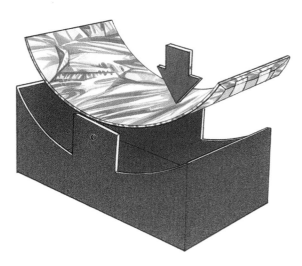

Pressure

Pressure is the name we give to the force that is exerted over an area by a solid, liquid or gas.

Propel

To propel something is to drive it forward.

Reservoir

A reservoir is an artificial lake or tank used for storing large quantities of water.

Temperature

Temperature is a measure of how hot or cold something is. The two most common temperature scales are Fahrenheit and Celsius.

Turbine

A turbine is a wheel with blades that are turned by a flow of gas or liquid.

Index

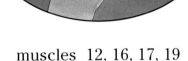